THE GREAT RIDDLE MYSTERY

by James R. MacLean
Illustrated by Leanne Franson

Modern Curriculum Press
Parsippany, New Jersey

ISBN 0-7652-0893-8

Printed in the United States of America

17 18 V031 12 11 10

1-800-321-3106
www.pearsonlearning.com

CONTENTS

CHAPTER 1
What Jody Saw

The last week in March was clear and cool. As Jody Martin headed for Quincy Park after school, she thought, "I'm glad I have soccer today, so I can warm up."

After 20 minutes of warm-ups, Coach Williams called, "We have just enough time for a practice game."

For the first half of the game, Jody, who was a goalie, blocked every kick. But as the afternoon light faded, she found it harder to see the ball. Finally, one ball flew over Jody's head and over the goal. It rolled toward the trees at the edge of the field.

"I'll get it!" Jody yelled to her teammates. She chased after the moving ball.

The ball rolled under a group of small fir trees. Jody bent down as she ran. She was looking under the low branches for any sign of the ball.

Suddenly, she saw something white through the trees. It was too big to be the ball, though. It also seemed to be glowing.

Jody stopped and peered through the branches. The white thing looked like a tall dome. "What can it be?" she thought.

Suddenly, a light flashed. It was so bright it hurt Jody's eyes. She covered her eyes, then peered through her fingers.

Two shapes appeared in front of the dome and started to walk toward her. They looked like people, but they walked stiffly. As they came closer, Jody saw that the shapes were shiny silver and had big round heads.

"What's happening?" Jody asked herself. She quickly looked around. She didn't see any other people or equipment.

The only other thing she could think of was an impossible idea. "Maybe it's from space," she thought. "It's an unidentified flying object. What's a UFO doing in Quincy Park?"

Suddenly, the light flashed again. Jody covered her eyes. Then a great whoosh of wind blew past her, and the light went out.

Without looking, Jody whirled around. As she ran, she thought, "The other girls are never going to believe me."

CHAPTER 2

Comparing Notes

Jody was right. No one on the team believed her. Instead they teased her for being afraid to go into the dark trees to find the ball. Coach Williams was kind and said that probably the dim light under the trees had played tricks on Jody's eyes.

Jody was angry. She was not the kind of person who was easily scared or who made things up.

The next morning, Jody picked up the
newspaper while she was eating breakfast.
She was amazed at what she read on the
front page. The headline read, "UFO Seen
in Quincy Park."

"Mom, Dad, did you see this story in the
newspaper?" she asked.

"Yes," her dad answered. "Isn't it silly?
People see something unusual, and
everybody thinks it's a UFO."

"Well, it is unidentified," Jody's mother said. "But everybody always thinks that 'unidentified' means an alien spacecraft."

"It says in the article that lots of people saw the UFO and called the police. Is that true, Mom?" Jody asked.

"Yes, it was crazy around the station for a while last night," her mom replied. Mrs. Martin was an officer on the Quincy police force. "The newspaper seems to know more than we do," she added.

When Jody got to school, she found out that her soccer teammates seemed to have told the whole school that Jody Martin said she saw a UFO in the park. She was hit with questions as soon as she came in the door. Jody felt a little angry at her teammates. They hadn't believed her yesterday.

Jody's friends Brad Ming, Tina Perez, and Ben Stubbs rescued her from the crowd.

"We all saw it, too!" Ben said excitedly.

"You saw the UFO?" Jody asked.

"Yes, I was walking the dog," Ben said.

"I was coming home from the store with some milk for my mom," Tina said.

"I was on my way to a Boy Scout meeting at school," Brad said. "*I* think it was just a UO. It wasn't flying. It was on the ground," he added.

"Let's talk about this after school," Jody said. She smiled for the first time that day.

After school the four friends hurried to Jody's house. They each told what they had seen in the park. They all agreed there had been a bright light. Ben had seen the silvery shapes too, but from farther away. Only Jody had felt and heard the great rush of wind.

"This is a real mystery!" Ben said.

"I bet we can solve it," Brad said.

"We were all in the park when it happened," Tina added. "So, we've already got some clues."

"What do you think, Mom?" Jody asked. Her mom was getting ready for work.

"If you kids are going to look into this mystery, you've got to be careful," Mrs. Martin said. "I'll see what I can find out at the station house."

"Thanks, Mrs. Martin," Tina said.

"It's very unlikely that this thing will turn out to be an alien spacecraft," Mrs. Martin added. "Most of these kinds of events end up having simple explanations."

"We know," Ben said. Then he turned back to the group. "Just think," he said, "what if it turns out to be a real UFO?" He loved mysteries and odd events.

CHAPTER 3
The First Riddle

The next day the four friends began asking their classmates what they had heard and seen. They each took notes.

Later that afternoon they met at Brad's house. They were each carrying copies of *The Quincy Times*. Brad's parents asked them all to stay for pizza.

They spread their newspapers out on the table. They began reading the articles and noting anything that could be a clue.

"Look at this," Jody said. She pointed to something on the page at the end of the UFO article. "What is this?"

Brad took the paper and read,

Can you solve this?
What catches a moment in time
and tells a story?

"It sounds like some kind of riddle to me," he said.

"I don't get it," Ben said. "What does 'a moment in time' mean?"

"Well, it's right at the end of today's story about the UFO," Jody pointed out. Everyone could see the headline "UFO Disappears in a Flash."

"The riddle doesn't seem to be part of the story," Tina added. "I think it's some kind of a newspaper contest."

Just then the doorbell rang. Mr. Ming thought it was the pizza.

Instead of someone holding a pizza box, there were two men standing there. One held a large camera. The other had a notebook and a small tape recorder.

"Good evening," said the man with the tape recorder. "My name is Reggie. This is Pete. We're from *The Quincy Times*."

Reggie looked over Mr. Ming's shoulder. "Are you Brad?" He waved at Brad.

"Yes," Brad said. "What do you want?"

"We've been asking around about this UFO business in the park. We heard that you have been asking a lot of questions, too," Pete said to Brad.

Reggie turned to Jody. "We heard you saw the flying saucer in the park," he said.

"We all saw it," Brad said. "And it wasn't flying."

"We're not even sure it was a saucer," Jody added.

"Did you see it up close?" Reggie asked.

"Close enough!" Tina said quietly.

A sudden flash made them jump. It was Pete, taking pictures.

"Just a minute!" Mr. Ming shouted.

"Where did you see the aliens?" asked Reggie.

"They were outside the dome," Jody answered. "But I'm not sure what they were."

"Did they get inside the spaceship?" Reggie asked. "Did you see the spaceship take off?"

"I'm not sure," said Ben.

Pete kept taking pictures until Mr. Ming stopped him. "I want both of you to leave now," he said sternly.

"What was that all about?" Jody asked.

"Sounds as if the newspaper is as interested as we are to find out what happened," Brad said.

"I think the only way we are going to find out more about this mystery, before the newspaper solves it, is to go back to the park and look around," Ben said.

"I wonder what we'll find," Tina added.

CHAPTER 4

The Park in the Dark

"You're not going to the park by yourselves," Mr. Ming said. "I'll go with you."

"Maybe my mom will go, too," Jody said. "She's probably home from work by now. She's not working the late shift tonight."

Jody called her mother while Brad and his father looked for some flashlights.

Mr. Ming and the kids met Officer Martin at the entrance to Quincy Park. The sun had just set. A chilly wind blew.

"It still feels like winter, even though it's spring," Jody said. "I can't believe it's almost April 1," she shivered.

"OK, let's go," Officer Martin said. "Jody, show us where you saw the UFO."

Jody led the group up a little hill. She stopped at the line of fir trees where she had lost the soccer ball.

"Keep your eyes open, everybody,"
Officer Martin said.

"All I see are grass and weeds," Brad
said.

"Hey! Look at this!" Jody called. "There's
the soccer ball." Everyone groaned as Jody
picked up the ball. "Well, Coach Williams
will be happy," she added.

"Listen!" Tina said. Everyone became
quiet. "I hear a trickling sound."

"It sounds like water," said Officer Martin.

They all pointed their flashlights at the ground, but the ground was completely dry.

"Look at this!" Ben said loudly. He held out something for the others to see.

Mr. Ming took it from him. "It's just a piece of an old balloon," he said.

"That's no help at all," Tina sighed.

"It's too dark to see anything now,"
Officer Martin said. "Let's go home."

They all turned to leave the park. No one
spoke. Everyone was getting grouchy.

Then, just as they were going out onto
the soccer field, Tina stopped. "Look!" she
shouted. "It's the UFO!"

They all stopped and looked. A bright
dome appeared through the trees.

At first, Jody thought the round object looked just like the UFO. But then, she saw their mistake. "It's just the moon," she said.

And it was. The moon was rising. It was a big, bright, full moon that looked huge through the trees.

"I *know* it wasn't the moon that I saw the other night," Jody said.

"We believe you," said Brad, Tina, and Ben.

CHAPTER 5

Riddles and Clues

They were discouraged by their wasted trip to the park. They wondered whether they would ever solve the mystery.

The four friends finally agreed they couldn't give up. So they decided to work on gathering their own clues.

Brad started with the newspaper. Every day he saved *The Quincy Times.* He cut out the articles about the UFO. Soon he had a group of headlines that read, "UFO Lands in Park!" "Aliens Have a Picnic in Quincy Park!" "Will the Aliens Return?" and "City to UFO: Now What?"

Brad also had several riddles. Monday's riddle was,

> *Floating all around the town,*
> *what goes up that must come down?*

On Tuesday he read,

> *Where in the wood does the holly tree grow?*

On Wednesday he found,

> *What is worth a thousand words?*
> *Solve this riddle and a prize is yours!*

Brad didn't know for sure, but he was beginning to think that the riddles had something to do with the UFO.

Tina found a clue on the way home from visiting her aunt, Tía Luisa. She and her family were riding the subway when suddenly the train slowed, then stopped.

A voice spoke over the loudspeaker. "Attention. We have track problems ahead. We'll be using the old Quincy line."

"What's the old Quincy line?" Tina asked.

"It runs under the park," said her father. "The station was closed because of water problems. An underground stream runs into the station."

Tina's father added, "They still use the tracks, though, when there's a problem."

"Can you still get to the station from the park?" she asked.

"The stairs are closed, but I think there is an entrance that workers use," he answered.

As the train slowly moved past the old, deserted station, Tina was thinking hard. "Running water," she thought. She remembered what she had heard the other night in the park.

While Tina was busy thinking about water and subway stations, Jody was on her way to Brad's house. She planned to help him with his little sister's birthday party.

They sat on the living-room floor, blowing up balloons. Brad was thinking so hard about the riddles that he wasn't watching how hard he was blowing. One of the balloons burst with a loud bang and a great *whoosh*!

Jody felt the rush of air against her face. It reminded her of something.

"That's it!" she exclaimed.

While Tina, Brad, and Jody worked on their clues, Ben was spending time in his room, thinking about the UFO. "I wish I had my camera that night," he thought. "Then I could have taken a picture."

Ben picked up his camera from his desk. As he was looking at it, he accidentally pushed the button. Suddenly, the flash went off right in his face.

For a few seconds, Ben couldn't see a thing. Then he remembered the night he had seen the UFO.

"There was a bright flash of light then, too!" he cried.

CHAPTER 6

Figuring It Out

Ben hurried to his classroom the next morning. He dashed over to his friends. "I think I've figured something out."

"I have, too," Tina said.

"Me too," Jody added.

"And me," Brad said.

Ben went first. "The night we saw the UFO, we saw the bright dome. Then we saw a flash, right?" he asked. Everyone nodded. "Well, last night I accidentally set off my camera flash. I couldn't see for a few seconds. It was just like in the park. Maybe it was a big camera flash. It was the kind of light that would give someone a chance to run away without anyone seeing."

"I saw the dome," Brad said. "How do you explain that?"

"I can explain it," Jody said. "I was
blowing up balloons with Brad last night.
One of the balloons burst. The sound and
the air coming out of that balloon made
me think of what I heard and felt that night
when the UFO disappeared."

"What balloon is that big?" Ben asked.

"It could have been a weather balloon,"
Jody said. "Remember that piece of
balloon we found?"

"Maybe some people could have done all that," said Brad, "but I don't think so. They would not have enough time. They would have to cross the field and set things up. Then they would have to get rid of all that stuff and get away."

"I think I know the answer to that one," Tina said. "What if they brought their stuff up from under the ground?" She told them her idea about the old subway station.

"But who would set up such a big joke?" Jody asked. "It would take a lot of work."

"What's the joke?" Ben asked.

"Someone is trying to make us think a UFO landed when it didn't," Tina replied.

"I have an idea who might have done it," Brad said. He held up *The Quincy Times*. The headline on the front page said, "Invasion Soon?" Brad pointed to the bottom where there was another riddle. *At what time of year is it cool to be a fool?* Then he pointed to the date, April 1. "Today is April Fools' Day," he explained.

CHAPTER 7
What They Found

At that moment, Ms. Ramos, their teacher, came over. She had overheard them talking about the UFO.

"Have you figured out something about this UFO?" she asked.

"We've almost got it figured out," the kids said. They told her about the clues they had put together.

"We've got to go back to the park," Ben said. "We should go tonight."

"Who's going with you?" asked Ms. Ramos.

"My mom will probably go with us," Jody said. "She's a police officer."

"And my dad, too," Brad added.

"I'd like to help," Ms. Ramos said. "But now it's time to get going on our math lesson."

That evening, Ms. Ramos came to the Martins' house. Mr. Ming, Brad, Tina, and Ben were already there.

"Are you saying that what you saw wasn't real?" Officer Martin asked Jody.

"It *was* real," Jody replied, "but it wasn't what it seemed. Someone fooled us. Someone made us *think* we saw a UFO."

"We still haven't figured out all the riddles," Brad said. "We're sure the riddles have something to do with the UFO."

"I think I may have some ideas on those riddles," Ms. Ramos said. "Two of the riddles were 'What catches a moment in time and tells a story?' and 'What is worth a thousand words?' When Ben talked about his camera going off, I thought those riddles could mean a camera flash and a photograph." Everyone agreed.

"Then when Jody talked about the
balloon, I thought about the riddle 'Floating
all around the town, what goes up that
must come down?'" Ms. Ramos continued.

"A balloon!" Jody said.

"But what does the other one mean,
'Where in the wood does the holly tree
grow?'" Brad asked.

"That's a hard one," Ms. Ramos replied.

"Let's go back to the park and find the subway entrance," Ben said. They all agreed.

It was dark by the time they got to Quincy Park. They all made sure their flashlights were working.

"Here are the rules," said Officer Martin. "Stay close together, and be careful. Call out if you see something."

They entered the park, walking as quietly as they could. Wind whistled through the trees, and the air smelled like rain. They heard a rumble of thunder. Moving as fast as they could, they soon reached the spot where the UFO had appeared.

"The old subway entrance is over here," Officer Martin said. They followed her to the spot. All they found were a couple of steps leading down to a brick wall.

"No one could get through there," Tina said, disappointed.

"Over here," Mr. Ming said. He was
standing by a cover over a raised area on
the ground. "I think it's the service
entrance to the subway."

"Help me lift the cover," Officer Martin
said to Mr. Ming. They both grabbed the
cover and got ready to lift.

"Wait!" Tina hissed. "Listen!" They all stopped and listened. Coming from under the ground were noises that sounded like voices. They were coming closer.

"Quick!" Officer Martin said. "Everyone hide!" She and Mr. Ming let go of the cover. Everyone ran into the bushes.

CHAPTER 8

Caught in the Act

Hiding in the bushes, they all turned off their flashlights. No one could see well.

Suddenly, the voices seemed to come from right under the cover. They all heard a clank as the cover began to lift.

"If you can just get it set up right, I can still take a picture. That should be enough," a voice said.

One man came up out of the ground, carrying a camera. Three men followed. Two of them were dressed in some kind of silver racing suit. They carried a heap of rubbery-looking cloth, two big photographer's floor lamps, hoses, a big metal tank, and two big helmets with visors.

"I know the guy with the camera. It's Pete from *The Quincy Times*," Brad whispered.

When the equipment was partly set up, Ben dashed out from behind his bush. He held up his camera and snapped three fast shots. The flashes lit up the whole place.

The men jumped in the blinding light.

"What's happening? Who are you?" Reggie yelped in surprise. He peered at Ben. "What are *you* doing here?" he asked.

"We want to know what *you* are doing here," Officer Martin said as she and everyone else came out from behind the bushes.

The men in the silver suits looked shocked. "Let's get out of here," they said.

Suddenly, everyone seemed to be running around. The men in the silver suits grabbed their equipment. Then, before anyone could get close enough to stop them, they ran off through the park. Reggie and Pete followed them.

"Oh, no," Tina cried. "They got away!"

"No, they didn't," Ben said. "I've got them right in here." He held up his camera.

The next day, Ms. Ramos took the film to a photo shop that had one-day service. She picked up the pictures after school and brought them to Jody's house. Brad, Tina, and Ben were already there.

Ms. Ramos laid the pictures on the table. "They're kind of fuzzy," she said. "We'll have a hard time proving who set up the UFO."

"Look!" Ben pointed to one of the pictures. "That's the tank the men had. It has writing on it."

Everyone examined the picture closely. "It says 'Metro Movie Studios,'" Jody read.

"It's the answer to the last riddle!" Brad cried. "Wood and holly could be Hollywood!"

"If they are going to make a movie," said Ms. Ramos, "this picture is proof."

"I think it's time we called the newspaper," Officer Martin said. "We'll get to the bottom of this mystery yet!"

She went to the phone and called. "I'd like to speak to a reporter named Reggie," she said. "Tell him I have proof of what the UFO in the park is all about."

CHAPTER 9
Winners!

They were right about the movie. When Reggie and Pete heard about the picture, they came right over to Jody's house.

"Those guys *are* from Metro Movie Studios," Reggie said. "They were trying to get people interested in a movie Metro plans to film here. They asked the newspaper to help them out. So we're running the articles about the UFO."

"A movie filmed in Quincy!" all the kids said together. "That's great!"

"Hold it!" Officer Martin said. "A lot of people have been worried about what's going on. When were you planning to let the rest of us in on the joke?" she asked.

"The head of movie publicity will be here at the end of the week. We planned to explain everything then," Reggie said.

"What about the riddles?" Brad wanted to know. "Are they part of this whole thing?"

"Yes," Reggie said. "We were going to announce the contest winner at the same time."

"Well, I think you'd better make that announcement now," Officer Martin said, pointing to Ben, Brad, Tina, and Jody.

That weekend, Tina's family held a big
party to celebrate solving the mystery. Mr.
Stubbs baked a big cake in the shape of a
flying saucer. Mrs. Perez brought out a big
bowl of fruit punch.

Brad came in, carrying a copy of *The
Quincy Times.* "Look at this, everyone!"

They all gathered around to see the
headline. It said, "Quincy Kids Win *Times*
Riddle Contest."

"Look!" Jody pointed to the bottom of
the page. "That's the photo that Ben took."

"So what did you win for solving the
mystery?" Mr. Perez asked.

"Well, we got our pictures in the newspaper," Ben said.

"Hey, everyone. I have something for you," Tina said, holding up a paper bag. She took out some gifts she had made. They were headsets with little wire antennas that had foam balls on the ends. When she put one on her head, the balls moved up and down.

"Look at me," she said. "I'm a space alien." Everyone laughed.

"Jody, tell everyone the best part," Officer Martin said.

"The person in charge of publicity for Metro Movie Studios called this morning," Jody began. "She wants us all to be extras in the movie."

"Wow! We're going to be in a movie!" Ben, Tina, and Brad all cheered.

"What stars are out in the daytime?" Jody asked.

"Movie stars!" the kids cried as Mr. Stubbs took their picture.

GLOSSARY

alien (AY lee un) a person from another place; a space alien would be from another planet

antennas (an TEN uz) a pair of movable feelers on an insect's head or a set of wires on a radio or television that sends and receives signals

dome (dohm) a round structure, such as a roof, that is shaped like half a ball or globe

extras (EKS truz) people hired to appear in a movie, usually as part of a crowd

photographer (fuh TAHG ruh fur) a person whose job it is to take pictures or photographs with a camera

publicity (pub LIHS uh tee) information that tells people about a person, a place, or an event, such as a movie

riddle (RIHD ul) a puzzle in the form of a question or a statement that has a tricky meaning or an answer that is hard to guess

shift (shihft) a period of time for work

subway (SUB way) an underground tunnel for trains

unidentified (un eye DEN tih fyd) not known or recognized